Amazon Mechanical Turk

Start to Make Money Online

Ines Mechler

Table of Contents

Disclaimer

While all attempts have been made to verify the information provided in this book, the author does assume any responsibility for errors, omissions, or contrary interpretations of the subject matter contained within. The information provided in this book is for educational and entertainment purposes only. The reader is responsible for his or her own actions and the author does not accept any responsibilities for any liabilities or damages, real or perceived, resulting from the use of this information.

The trademarks that are used are without any consent, and the publication of the trademark is without permission or backing by the trademark owner. All trademarks and brands within this book are for clarifying purposes only and are the owned by the owners themselves, not affiliated with this document. **

Introduction

Most countries in the world are facing unemployment. This calls for those looking for employment to seek alternative sources of income. Online jobs are becoming a common source of income for many people in most countries. Who are you to be left out? With online jobs, you can earn a lot while working from your house. The Amazon Mechanical Turk is one of the best sites where one can get online jobs. Most of the jobs in this site do not require any professional qualifications. This book guides you on how to earn money from the Amazon Mechanical Turk. Enjoy reading!

Chapter 1- What is Mechanical Turk?

This is a service provided by Amazon where one can complete some simple tasks and get some tiny payments. A simple task may be looking at an image and describing it, and you will be paid some amount of money, based on the number of tasks completed. It can be seen as a marketplace which needs human intelligence for operations. In most cases, the tasks available in the Mechanical Turk are very easy.

This gives businesses an access to a pool of workers and the workers are given a chance to select the best work from a variety of available tasks. These are the tasks which computers are unable to do. As an employer, you have to post your job as a Human Intelligent Task (HIT).

The workers are then expected to browse among the list of available jobs, complete them, and they will in turn be paid for their services. For an individual who needs to post their job on the Amazon Mechanical Turk, they have to provide Amazon with their billing address.

Chapter 2- Account Setup

For you to be able to use the Amazon Mechanical Turk, you should first sign up for an Amazon Web Services (AWS) account. This is just an account with the Amazon.com, and will allow you to use the services of AWS. The following steps are necessary for you to sign up for an AWS account:

1. On your browser, open aws.amazon.com and then choose "Create an AWS Account."

2. You will then be taken through a sequence of steps in which you will be required to add your details so as to create the account. Follow these instructions so as to create an account. You will also get a phone call from Amazon, and you will be prompted to enter a pin number via your phone keypad. You will then be done!

However, it is good for you to know that the credentials, that is, the username and the password you use in your AWS account have to be the same credentials you use in your Amazon Mechanical Turk account. With that account, it will be possible for you to view all the activity that you carry out in it and manage the security credentials for your account.

During access to the AWS account, access keys are normally used for the protection of your data. The access key is made up of an access key id and a secret access key. The access key id can be seen as a username, while the secret access key can be seen as a password. For you to make a request to the Amazon Mechanical Turk, you have to sign it by use of the access keys.

The Security Credentials

It is good for you to manage the security credentials for your AWS account. This can be done as follows:

1. Sign in to your AWS account. Navigate to the security credentials page. If you had logged in as an IAM user, select the "Access Keys." Of course, these are the access key ID and the secret key we discussed earlier. If you had used the root credentials to login, click on "Continue to Security Credentials."

2. Click on "Create New Access Key," and then click on "Download Key File."

This will download the rootkey.csv file into your browser, and this is a private key file. Copy this file and save it in a secure place.

The Requester Account

For you to be able to use the Mechincal Turk, you must have created a Requester account. The following steps can help you create your Requester account:

1. Open **https://requester.mturk.com** and select "Create an Account."

2. You can type in your email address. Ensure that you use the same credentials that you used to create a root AWS account. You will also be prompted to provide your details through a series of screens. Ensure that you fill them in as expected and you will be done. The email address should be the appropriate one and ensure that you agree to the terms.

The IAM User

IAM stands for Identity and Access Management. It can help one control how users get access to their resources. Once you have created an IAM user, you will be able to use the credentials so as to access your AWS Mechanical Turk account, rather than having to use your root account credentials. The following steps can help you create an IAM user:

1. Sign to your account for Amazon Web Services (AWS), and then navigate to the security credentials page.

2. Click on "Get Started with IAM Users," and then click on "Create New Users."

3. Type in the names for your users. Also, you should ensure that you have generated an access key for each of your users. After that, click on "Create."

4. Click on "Show User Security Credentials." Click on "Download Credentials."

Your browser will download the private key file, which is credentials.csv, so ensure that you save it in a safe place.

Permissions are of importance when it comes to the use of the AWS resources and the Amazon Mechanical Turk resources. The permissions will determine the kind of resources that the user can access, as well as the kind of activities that they can do. Of course, you don't want the users to be able to do anything which may destroy your account, and this can only be done by implementing permissions.

The permissions for IAM users in an Amazon Mechanical Turk account can be set as follows:

1. Open the IAM console, and then sign into it. This can be found at

https://console.aws.amazon.com/iam/home#policies.

2. Navigate to the page for "Policies," and then choose "AmazonMechanicalTurkReadOnly" or the "AmazonMechanical TurkFullAccess."

3. Select "Policy Options" from the top of the page, and then select "Attach." Navigate to the page for "Attach Policy," choose your IAM users who you need to set the permissions for. Select "Attach Policy and the users will be granted permission so as to be able to gain access to the Mechanical Turk API.

That is it! However, so far, we have not installed the SDK for the Amazon Mechanical Turk together with the necessary tools. It provides us with some command line tools and SDKs which make our work easier. This calls for you to install one of the command line tools or one of the available SDKs.

If you need to use the command line, you should first install the command line tools, and then configure them correctly.

For Windows users, the following steps can help you:

1. Download the command line tools from the command line tools page for the Amazon Mechanical Turk.

2. Double click on the mech-turk-setup.exe file so as to run it. Follow the instructions presented to you to perform the installation.

The following steps can help you do this in Unix systems:

1. Open the Amazon Mechanical Turk on your browser and navigate to the page with command line tools.

2. Navigate to the directory for installation of the command line tools. Find the file named "Overview.html," and then open it. This file should be

the one to guide you on how to install and then configure the command line tools. Kindly follow the steps within the file so as to do this.

Also, you have to remember your security credentials, as they will be needed for you to complete the steps. You can choose to use either the security credentials for your IAM user account or the ones for your AWS account.

After that, you will have completed the installation for the command line tools. You should go ahead and configure it so that it can make use of the credentials of the IAM. The following steps can help you do this:

1. Open the CLI folder, and then navigate to the /bin directory. Find the file named mturk.properties and then open it.

2. You can then set the secret key and the access key so that they can match those of the IAM.

Chapter 3- The Scripts

As a worker on Amazon Mechanical Turk, you will be working on the Human Intelligent Tasks (HITs). However, for those who have done this before, you might have experienced some little inconveniences. The extra clicks which most pages need usually slow workers.

The purpose of the Amazon Mechanical Turk scripts is to increase the wage that you earn per hour by shaving seconds off between your times each HIT. The fact is that scripts are designed by individual people for solving a particular problem. Whenever an individual experiences a problem on the MTurk, they usually go ahead and create a script which can solve the problem. Most scripts come with a plugin which helps to work with it, meaning that it is not a must for you to learn how to write the code.

Before you can install scripts into your browser, you should first find and install some extensions.

For those who are using Firefox as their browser, begin by installing GreaseMonkey. This will allow you to customize your browser to the way you need it to behave. You will use some small JavaScript code and customize the way content will be displayed on your browser. Find it online, and download it. Note that you can use this extension for free.

If you are using Chrome as your browser, then install the TamperMonkey. This extension will also help you to customize the way your Chrome browser displays content.

Installing the Scripts

Now that you have the extension which is necessary for your browser, you can go ahead to install the MTurk scripts. You should understand that the scripts will be added to the GreaseMonkey and the TamperMonkey. You will not be expected to do anything, as this will be done automatically on your behalf.

Also, it is good for you to use the browser in which you want to load the script. The installation of the extensions could have been done in both browsers if you have them, and repeat the same to install the scripts. After the installation is complete, you will not notice it, but once you get to the Mechanical Turk website, you will know it. You will see them on the MTurk web pages, and they will automatically begin to do their job.

The following are some of the MTurk scripts which can help to make your work easier:

1. Turkopticon

   This is a very useful script. Of course, you will be working for a particular Requester. It is good for you to learn more about them so as to choose the best ones. This script will let you learn what the rest of the workers think about the Requester who you are working for. You will also have a chance to rate the Requesters on MTurkey, and this will help other workers learn more about him or her. Turkopticon comes with a version for Chrome and another version for Firefox.

2. Block Requesters

   As you work on MTurk, you will come across Requesters who you will never want to work for again. In such a case, you may need to hide the HITs from them. This may be because the Requester pays poorly, or maybe because they have been receiving bad reviews for a long time. In such a case, this script will help you hide all their HITs or in other words, you block them. It also comes with the script for Chrome and another one specific to Firefox.

3. Show Captcha and Accept Button

   Some people do not like waiting for the accept button and the captcha to be loaded simply because they hate this. If you belong to this category, then you can choose to speed up how fast these are loaded. This script will help you with this. Just install it and you wull enjoy its benefits.

4. Block Individual Requests

   Are there some HITs which you don't need to see? Once you install this script, you will see some text labeled "View a HIT in this group" at the end of this line. Once you click on the X, this HIT will be hidden from you and you will not see it again. Of course, this will save you time when you are searching for tasks to complete and earn something, meaning that you will have increased your pay per hour.

5. TurkMaster

   This is a very good tool, and very helpful once you have learned how to use it. It works by adding some filters to the left of your web page. Once you have activated any filter, the script will alert you about it. Of course, you will need to work more for your favorite Requester so as to earn more. With this script, you can allow it to alert you whenever your favorite Requester has created a HIT. Also, it can inform you whenever a high-paying HIT has been listed. Note that there are qualification levels in MTurk. Requesters usually specify the qualifications they need from workers when posting their HITs. You can configure this script to inform you whenever a HIT in need of a certain qualification level is created. The settings can also be changed so that you can also receive the notifications even when you are working. However, for you to keep on getting the notifications, you have to keep a separate tab which should be running on your account page.

6. HIT Scraper WITH EXPORT

   When searching for the best HITs, it is good for you to sort them so that the best ones can be listed first. In such a case, this script helps you to achieve it. Although you may have to spend some time before you learn it, you will definitely enjoy it once you learn how to use it.

7. MTurk Dashboard Change Notifier

   This is a great addition to your MTurk account page. It will track the changes of the 12 different values since your last time refreshing the page. These are a number of statistics such as earnings, bonuses, HITs status, and the amount transferrable. It will be possible for you to note any changes without having to do some math. Again, this script comes in versions for both Chrome and Firefox.

8. Time Tracker

   This script will help you track the amount of time that you spend while working on HITs to the amount of money that you earn. With this kind of information, you will be able to know the amount of dollars that you earn per hour. The timer has to be started manually once you start working and then you stop it manually once you are done with the work. If you fail to do this, you will end up getting the wrong results.

9. MTurk Hit DB

   With this script, you will be able to keep track of the HITs which you have completed. The amount you have earned will also be tracked and kept in a database. It has other additional functionalities such as blockage of Requesters, showing of projected earnings, showing of pending earnings and be showing the time of auto approval for a particular HIT.

Those are some of the scripts which you can install, and they will make your work on MTurk easier. This will in turn translate into more earnings. But you may ask yourself, are the scripts secured?

Most scripts developed for the MTurk are secure. Many users usually test them, and they then give feedback regarding how they work. The fact is that some scripts can be harmful. You should always remember that the scripts are created by people, and they may need to be malicious for different reasons. A script is nothing but just instructions which tells your computer how to treat or display content on your web pages.

However, the good thing is that the Firefox and Chrome browsers will limit the capabilities of the script, reducing the number of tasks that it can do, and this will help keep you safe. The scripts also lack great power like the scripts and extensions which come with your browser. Some people may create scripts which will capture the data you type on the browsers and then send it to them. This is why you should do thorough research about a particular script before you can go ahead to install it on your browser.

Research for information about the number of users who have used the script and check for any ratings and reviews which the users might have given about it. This will let you lea whether the script is bad or not. If there are bad ratings and reviews, then it will be safe for you to forget about it. A script with a high number of users, good comments, and good ratings is the best one, so look for such. Also, some websites, including the Amazon Mechanical Turk, are very secure and they will warn you whenever they sense something dangerous with your MTurk account. Learn not to ignore such warnings.

Chapter 4- The HIT Scrapper

This is a good tool which helps MTurk workers to find HITs. The tool is very easy for anyone to use, and it provides us with the most effective way to find HITs. For you to install and use this tool, you must have installed the extensions we installed in our previous chapter, that is, Greasemonkey for Firefox and Tampermonkey for Chrome. After you have installed these extensions, go to the HIT Scrapper website and then install it by clicking on “install this script.”

Once the tool has been installed, you will have to open the link given below on MTurk:

https://www.mturk.com/mturk/findhits?match=false&hit_scraper

You will then have accessed the HIT scrapper from MTurk, and this will load it but with the default setting. The first thing should be adjustment of the settings.

- Change the property “Auto-refresh delay” to the speed that you want to have, like 10 seconds. This setting will determine how new HITs will be scrapped.

- Change the value of “Pages to scrape” to 1.

- Change the value of 'Results per page' to a reasonable value, like 20 or 50. Although this property takes a maximum value of 100, do not set it too high, as it will cause a lag.

- Adjust the value of minimum reward or retain it at 0. However, if you wish to change it, give it another value, or leave it at 1.00 in case you only need the higher paying surveys. However, before setting this, it is good for you to know that any HITS which pay less than the threshold you have set will not show in your HIT scraper. You can also choose to scrape only the HITs which you are qualified for.

- The property for minimum batch size is only important when you are intending to work on batches but avoid the surveys. This can be set to show only HITs with at least 50 HITs in a batch. To enable searching by the latest HITs, you have to tick the "global" option.

- The option for new HIT highlighting represents the number of seconds a HIT will be highlighted after it pop ups on the HIT scraper for the first time. The tool also provides you with an option which can help you ping any new HITs which may come. This is a nice setting, especially if you don't need to keep on looking at the HIT scrapper.

If you have the correct settings, or the ones that you desire to have, you can click on start. The “Hide Panel” will help you to hide the settings as you continue to use the scrapper. You are also provided with an option for adding an include list and a block list into the scrapper. Once you click on the “R” box, you will be able to include some Requesters to the block list. This means that you will not be able to see the HITs that they create on MTurk. The title of the HIT can also be blocked by clicking on “T” box which is found in the Requester column. However, once you do this, you will just have blocked the HIT but not the Requester, meaning that you will be able to see other HITs by the Requester.

Also, the Requesters can also be blocked by clicking on “Edit Blocklist” and then adding them one by one.

Chapter 5- MTurk PandA

This is a script which helps workers on MTurk to grab HITs as fast as possible. This script has now been evolved, and one can use it to accomplish much. It can help one do a pantha and this greatly helps workers in throttled batches. One can also use it to search for the HITs which are posted by a particular Requester. It has the GoHam button which will help grab HITs as soon as they are posted. In case it gets PRE's, which can help out whenever you try to work from the queue, it will begin to slow down. There is also list of your HITs in your current queue on the bottom so you can always know what's in your queue. The current queue will also have a list of HITs located at the bottom, and this will inform you of what you have in your queue.

It is also recommended that you run Panda on its own window. This is because the browsers have an effect of limiting your scripts to a timer of 1 second in case they are opened in an unfocused tab. However, if you need help on how to use Panda, you can get it online. It also comes with its own help, so you can take advantage of that in case of any difficulty. The alarms in the script can be changed to what you need.

This script also comes with some add-on scripts which can be of help when you are working on MTurk. They include the following:

1. Mturk Panda Crazy Helper- this will show some add buttons when you are on mturk.com and you will be able to send some projected earnings to the Panda Crazy main script.

2. Mturk Panda Crazy Queue Helper- this is a script which will go to your next lowest time hit in the queue. It will grab the data for the queue from the Panda Crazy rather

than having to send a request to MTurk after every submit. This will work so as to lead to reduced PRE's. This only works when the Panda Crazy main script is being run on a similar browser.

How to Integrate LimeSurvey with MTurk

The LimeSurvey is written in JQuery and PHP. A server will also be required for hosting purposes.

Let us begin by installing and configuring the LimeSurvey, and then we will test whether this is working correctly.

Begin by downloading and installing the latest version of wampserver. Download and then extract the LimeSurvey. Move it while unzipped to the www directory of the wampserver you have installed. After that, open your browser and then browse to **http://localhost/limesurvey**. This will help begin the installation of lLimeSurvey, so just begin to follow the steps.

After the installation of the LimeSurvey, go ahead and login as the admin. The I/p values are usually stored in your config.php file in the root directory of the LimeSurvey. The default login credentials are the admin/password. The following are our expectations from LimeSurvey:

1. Read the URL's assignmentId parameter. This represents part of URL which is added by Mechanical Turk to any of the HIT pages it is referring to.

2. Have the assignmentId stored as one of answers to questionnaire.

3. Refer workers who have finished the questionnaire to some confirmation link, which will add them to a list of people who should be considered for payment.

The following are the necessary steps:

1. Change the Global settings of LimeSurvey at \ Security \ Filter HTMl for the XSS to No.

2. Create a new Questions Group, Survey, and Question. Open the edit question screen. Set the type of the question to "Short free text," but if you need something different, set it to something else. The next step should be picking some Question Code now, which has to be anything which was not used in the survey.

3. Click on your Source button. After that, the rich-text editing will be disabled, and anything printed will be treated as raw code which should be added into your questionnaire.

4. Now that you have clicked on the Source button, add the code given below:

```
<script type="text/javascript">

function getUrlVars() {
var vars = new Array();
var parts =
window.location.href.replace(/[?&]+([^=&]+)=
([^&]*)/gi,
function(m,key,value) {
      vars[key] = value;
  });
  return vars;
}
//$(document).ready(function() {

$('#{SGQ}').val(getUrlVars()["yourQuestionCo
de"]);
//});
</script>
<style type="text/css">
#question{assignmentId.qid}{
```

display: none;

}

</style>

5. Open the survey's page for Edit survey text elements. Scroll down to the End URL field. Enter the following URL:

http://www.google.com/search?q={yourQuestionCode}

http://workersandbox.mturk.com/mturk/externalSubmit?finished=true& yourQuestionCode ={ yourQuestionCode }

Customizing it further

- You should be aware that a specific value is needed. This is assigned by the Mechanical Turk. I have called it "yourQuestionCode," so ensure that you replace this value with the question code which was assigned to you. Each system will have a different value for this, so use the correct value.

- Once the script tag has been closed, the next will be the style tag. If you choose question1 and then you make it invisible, the user will not be in a position to change the value which was assigned.

- You can then use the macro in your End URL which will help you include collected code in your reference URL to the confirmation page of Mechanical Turk. There is a better way that you can make this work with the auto-forwarding feature of JavaScript. This is also an indication that the code will be stored together with the results for the survey. The following points are worth noting:

- LimeSurvey makes use of lots of JQuery, and that is why you see the $ selectors in the code.
- Our first suggestion was to execute the code as being part of the custom document. Ready function.

We can place the function which is to parse the URL variables.

Chapter 6- AutoHotKey for Turking

AutoHotKey (AHK) is a free and open-source automation and macro-creation tool used in Windows to allow users make repetitive tasks automatic. AHK was created by use of a scripting language so as to provide some keyboard shortcuts, which are known as hotkeys, and these finally evolved into a full-fledged scripting language.

Before you can begin to use this script, you have to first download and then install it. The installer is the best way for you to get AHK working on your machine. This is what we will use in this case. The installation can be done by following the steps given below:

1. Open the **homepage** for the Autokey.

2. Download AHK by clicking on the download link.

3. As the installation continues, they will prompt to choose either the ANSI or the UNICODE versions. This means that it is capable of supporting non-English numbers and letters. Progresses until you see the install button. After some time, you will be done, and this is the time for you to proceed to the section b.

Creating a script

The fact is that the AHK tool is not automatic. This means that we have to give it instructions which will tell it what to do. This process is referred to as “scripting”. In AHK, scripts can be created as follows:

1. Right-Click on the desktop. Move to the menu and find "New."

2. Click the "AutoHotkey Script" located inside "New" menu.

3. Give a name to the script, noting that the name has to end with an .ahk extension. Example, OurScript.ahk

4. Move to the desktop, and find the file which has been created. Right-Click on the file. Click on "Edit Script."

5. You will see a window pop up, and most probably, it will be a notepad window. If this happens, you will have succeeded.

After that, you will have created a script file, and the next step should involve addition of some code to it. Let us write a basic script, which will have a hotkey for typing some text by use of the Send command once the hotkey has been pressed. Here is the script:

```
^j::
  Send, Our First Script
Return
```

The first line with ^j stands for ctrl, j, and j is a letter. The character represents the need to press. In the second line of the script, we are representing how hotkeys are sent. The command in this case is SEND, and everything written after the comma (,) will be typed. The last line in the script has the Return command. This will prevent the script from going any further. The command is very important and especially in cases where your script has a lot of code, as it will prevent you from a number of issues.

Now that you have added the script to the file, go ahead and save it. You can then run it by double clicking on it from the desktop. You just have to open Notepad and then type ctrl and then j (ctrl + j). You will have your script running! Congrats!

There are a number of ways that you can access the help file on your computer. Let us discuss some of the ways, as these will be helpful to you:

1. Open the desktop.

2. Open My Computer or Computer.

3. Open the harddrive with AutoHotkey. This is most probably the C:\ drive.

4. Search for AutoHotKey within all the Program Files folders.

5. Look for the AutoHotkey.chm or the file which says AutoHotkey with a yellow question mark. You will then be done!

This is the second method to accomplish this:

1. Find Start Orb or Start menu on the screen, usually located in the lower left.

2. Click on All Programs or Programs.

3. Find AutoHotkey from the list. You will see the AutoHotkey Help File. Just click it and you will be done!

With AHK, it will be easy for you to answer the HITs on MTurk. You can make some of your best search terms automatic or make a key press a way of filling out a form.

If you need the abbreviation which you may type, you can use the hotstrings. Hotstrings can also be used for the purpose of launching any scripted action. Here is an example of a hotsrting:

::hih::Here is a hotstring

The difference between the two is that your hotstring will be invoked once you type CTRL & J, while the hih will be translated to mean “Here is a hotstring.”

Now, the question is, how can one create a hotkey on their own? To create a hotkey, we use a single key, that is, ::'s. Your key or key combo will need to move to the left of: The content should then be added below this, followed by the Return statement.

It is good for you to remember that exceptions do exist, but these usually create some problems in most cases. The following example demonstrates this:

```
esc::
  MsgBox Escape
Return
```

It is good for you to remember that a hotstring should have some pair of::'s on the sides of the text which you need to invoke your text replacement. The text which you need to use for replacement of the typed text should be placed to the right of second pair of the:'s.

Hotstrings can also be used for launching scripted actions. This also applies to the hotkeys. This is shown below:

```
::jkl::
  MsgBox You have typed "jkl".
Return
```

It is also good for you to be aware that it is possible for you to write multiple lines for a single hotkey, label, hotstring. Consider the following example which demonstrates how this can be implemented:

```
^j::
  MsgBox Hello!
  MsgBox this is
  Run, Notepad.exe
  winactivate, Untitled - Notepad
  WinWaitActive, Untitled - Notepad
  send, 7 lines{!}{enter}
  sendinput, inside the ctrl{+}j hotkey
```

Return

Hotkeys and Hotstrings specific to Windows

In some cases, one may need a particular hotkey or hotstring to work only in a specific window. If this is what you want to achieve, then you have to use the following commands, and place a # symbol at their front:

#IfWinActive

#IfWinExist

These commands are known as directives, and they work by creating context-sensitive hotstrings and hotkeys. You just have to specify a title for the window. In other cases, you may be expected to specify some HWND, group, or a class. They are a bit advanced. Consider the example given below:

#IfWinActive Untitled - Notepad

#space::

MsgBox You have pressed Win+Spacebar in your Notepad.

Return

#IfWinActive

If you need to turn off the sensitivity of the context, you can specify any of the #IfWin commands, but ensure that the parameters are left empty. Consider the example given below:

; NOTEPAD

#IfWinActive untitled - Notepad

!q::

MsgBox, You have pressed the Alt and Q in your Notepad.

Return

#IfWinActive

; ANY WINDOW THAT ISN'T UNTITLED - NOTEPAD

!q::

MsgBox, You pressed Alt and Q in any window.

Return

Once you turn off all the #IfWin commands, all the hotstrings and the hotkeys will be enabled for all the windows. You have to note that the commands are positional, meaning that all the hotstrings and the hotkeys below them in the script will be affected. Consider the example given below:

; NOTEPAD

#IfWinActive ahk_class Notepad

#space::

MsgBox, You have pressed Win+Spacebar in your Notepad.

Return

::msg::The msg was typed in Notepad

#IfWinActive

; MSPAINT

#IfWinActive untitled - Paint

#space::

```
  MsgBox, You have pressed Win+Spacebar in your MSPaint!
Return
::msg::The msg was typed in MSPaint!
#IfWinActive
```

It is also possible for you to create multiple hotkeys or hotstrings for each file. With an AutoHotKey, it is possible for you to have as many hotstrings and hotkeys as you may need in a single file. This is shown below:

```
#i::
  run, http://www.google.com/
Return

^p::
  run, notepad.exe
Return

~j::
```

```
  send, ack
Return

:*:acheiv::achiev
::achievment::achievement
::acquaintence::acquaintance
:*:adquir::acquir
::aquisition::acquisition
:*:agravat::aggravat
:*:allign::align
::ameria::America
```

The code given has multiple hotstrings and multiple hotkeys, and it is accepted. Consider the next example given below:

::wba::Welcome back again ; REPLACES "WBA" WITH "WELCOME BACK AGAIN" ;ONCE YOU HIT AN ENDCHAR.

:*:wba::By the way ; REPLACES "WBA" WITH "WELCOME BACK AGAIN"WITHOUT ;THE NEED FOR AN ENDCHAR

^n:: ; CTRL & N HOTKEY

run, notepad.exe ; WILL RUN PROGRAM NOTEPAD.EXE ONCE YOU HIT CTRL & N

Return ; THIS WILL END HOTKEY. WE WILL NOT TRIGGER THE CODE BELOW THIS.

^b:: ; CTRL & B HOTKEY

send, {ctrl down}c{ctrl up} ; WILL COPY THE SELECTED TEXT. YOU CAN AS ;WELL USE ^C, BUT THIS IS A MORE SECURE METHOD.

SendInput, [b]{ctrl down}v{ctrl up}[/b] ; THIS WILL WRAP THE SELECTED TEXT ;IN THE BBCODE BOLD TAGS.

Return ; THIS WILL END THE HOTKEY.

;ANY BELOW THIS WILL NOT BE TRIGGERED

How to Send Keystrokes

You have decided to type or send keys in the program. This can easily be done by use of the "Send" command. Once this command is used, it sends keystrokes, meaning that the keys are simulated as you type them.

The following are some of the common symbols which are used in this:

1. !- this is used for sending the ALT key. Example, *Send I am good!x*. This will send the text "I am good," and then press the ALT+x keys. You have to remember that the! X would give different results in some systems like ALT+SHIFT+X, which is not the result we get from! x. If you are not sure of what the result will be, it is recommended that you use it in lowercase.

2. + will send the SHIFT key. Example, SEND +ABZ will send the text "AbZ," and SEND!+A will press ALT+SHIFT+a.

3. ^: will send CONTROL (Ctrl) key. Example, SEND ^!A will ess CTRL+ALT+a, while SEND ^{HOME} will send CONTROL+HOME. ^A gives a different resultt in some programs than ^a. The ^A presses the CONTROL+SHIFT+A while the ^a will press CONTROL+a. If you are not sure of the result, use a lowercase.

4. #: will Send the WIN key (key having Windows logo), hence SEND #E will hold down the Windows key and press the letter "e".

The following example shows how this can be done with a hotkey:

```
; MAKE A HOTKEY...

; WRONG

{LCtrl}::

  send, AutoHotkey

Return


; CORRECT

LCtrl::

  send, AutoHotkey

Return
```

Chapter 7- Turkmaster

In this chapter, we will discuss how one can install Turkmaster and use it in MTurk. For Firefox users, ensure that you have installed the Greasemonkey extension, and for Chrome users, ensure that you install Tampermonkey. You can then download Turkmaster, and install it. Ensure that you download its latest version.

After that, navigate to the dashboard and you will see a new column on your left. In case you don't like the default HITs/Requesters which are available, place the mouse over an entry in your list of the watched Requesters who you like so as to delete. You will see a pencil and some gray x,. Just click on that x and the entry will be deleted.

After that, go ahead and open a new tab. In this tab, search for the Requester who you would like to watch. If you see their HITs, just click on the name of the Requester and you will be taken to their page. A gray bubble will be presented and this will say, “Watch this requester?” If you need to add the Requester to the Turkmaster list, just click on that. For this to work, you must have opened your dashboard in the tab. It is possible for you to set the amount of time taken between checks for the HITs by the Requester, and you will choose whether to be alerted with a notification window or not. This can be done continuously for any Requester you need to watch.

If you need to use Turkmaster for searching for the HITs, just open your dashboard. You will be presented with two options: a double arrow button which starts ALL of the watches at a go, and an arrow with a square which starts only the ones where there exists a checkmark in your box on the watch. The checkbox can be found under the arrow on the left of the items in the list.

If you only need to search for one Requester at a time, you just have to click on the start arrow for each of the items. The dashboard also has the Pause icon which is located at the top. If you need to pause the watches, you just have to click on this icon. It is located next to the arrow with a square and the double arrow.

Once you click on the gear icon, you will be able to change the volume. It will also help to set whether the notifications should be displayed on the browser, the size of the font, and whether it will be possible to hide the user interface or not.

The same menu also has the Export (backup function). It is recommended that you make a backup on a weekly basis or in case you have made a change. This menu will help you do the backup in cases where you are fixing a new computer or doing some repair on an existing one.

In case an alert goes off, based on your settings, an audio alert or a notification will be sent to you and you will see it at the bottom right of the screen. The sound will not go on forever, and the window will not stay on for a long time, so it will be good for you to be vigilant. After the triggering of the alert, just open the Dashboard, and you will be able to see the HITs which are available. You will also observe the gray box having a white arrow which points to the right turn into green. This can be found on the right of each of the item which is in the watch list.

Just move your mouse to the top of that box, and you will see all the HITs which are available. You will be presented with four choices.

The “Preview” option is just a link which will help you to preview the HIT. The “Accept” option is a link which will help you accept a HIT, while the “+Auto” option will help you add the HIT to the watch list. It will also go ahead to accept more in case more appear, However, it is good for you to be careful with this as it will accept a HIT at any time, meaning that you may end up with a filled queue if you are not careful. Although this is good, it becomes bad for a shorter timer. The option for “Mute” is an indication that you will not be indicated for the HIT in the future. Be cautiousbefore you choose this, as it can make you miss some very important HITs.

In case you need to stop a HIT from alerting you, just click on the “Pause” icon which is located on the left of the item in the watchlist. It is also possible for one to add search words and phrases to the list, and an example of such a phrase is “survey.” You just have to search for that phrase or word on MTurk and then click on that “Watch this page?” located in the grey bubble of your search page. That is it!

Chapter 8- The SearchHITs Operation

This operation gives all the HITs for a particular Requester. All the HITs of all types are returned, except the ones which have gone through the DisposeHIT operation for disposing them off. The auto-disposed ones will also not be shown.

Oncrrre the operation is done; its result will be sorted and then grouped into pages. A single page of results will be returned by the operation. Parameters can be passed to the operation so as to control the process of sorting and pagination.

If you set the (*PageNumber* x *PageSize*) to a value which is less than 100, reliable results will be obtained even after using any type of the sort properties. In case you set this to a value which is greater than 100, then we recommend that you use the sort property named "Enumeration." With this, the HITs will be returned without duplicates, but the problem is that no order will be followed in presenting these.

The Parameters

This operation takes in some parameters. However, there are some common parameters which are always required. The following are some of the common request parameters for this operation:

1. Operation- this is the name of the operation, and it is required.

2. SortProperty- is the column based on which the results will be sorted, and it is not a must include.

3. SortDirection- this refers to the sort direction and it is not required.

4. PageSize- this refers to the number of HITs which are to be included in your page of results.

Those are the parameters for the request. The response should take the following parameters:

1. NumResults- this refers to the HITS on a page after filtering.

2. PageNumber- this represents the page number in the list of filtered results.

3. TotalNumResults- a non-negative integer which represents the HITs number after filtering based on the call.

4. HIT- this refers to the HIT element.

Consider the sample request given below:

https://mechanicalturk.amazonaws.com/?Service=AWSMechanicalTurkRequester

&AWSAccessKeyId=*[the Access Key IDof the Requester]*

&Operation=SearchHITs

&Signature=*[signature for request]*

&Timestamp=*[local time for the system]*

Here is an example of a sample response:

<SearchHITsResult>

<Request>

<IsValid>True</IsValid>

</Request>

<NumResults>3</NumResults>

<TotalNumResults>2</TotalNumResults>

<PageNumber>1</PageNumber>

<HIT>

<HITId>HBGZVQY4EHXZ1AYCY1T2</HITId>

<HITTypeId>MYYZTQ3QVYJZGCYXCYVX</HITType Id>

<CreationTime>2016-09-08T00:16:21Z</CreationTime>

```
<Title>Location</Title>
<Description>Choose here</Description>
<HITStatus>Reviewable</HITStatus>
<MaxAssignments>1</MaxAssignments>
<Reward>
 <Amount>10.00</Amount>
 <CurrencyCode>USD</CurrencyCode>
 <FormattedPrice>$10.00</FormattedPrice>
</Reward>
<AutoApprovalDelayInSeconds>2592000</AutoApprovalDelayInSeconds>
<Expiration>2016-09-08T00:16:21Z </Expiration>
<AssignmentDurationInSeconds>30</AssignmentDurationInSeconds>
<NumberOfAssignmentsPending>0</NumberOfAssignmentsPending>
<NumberOfAssignmentsAvailable>0</NumberOfAssignmentsAvailable>
<NumberOfAssignmentsCompleted>1</NumberOfAssignmentsCompleted>
```

</HIT>

<HIT>

<HITId> HBGZVQY4EHXZ1AYCY1T2</HITId>

<HITTypeId> MYYZTQ3QVYJZGCYXCYVX </HITTypeId>

<CreationTime>2016-09-08T00:16:21Z</CreationTime>

<Title>Location</Title>

<Description>Choose here</Description>

<HITStatus>Assignable</HITStatus>

<MaxAssignments>1</MaxAssignments>

<Reward>

<Amount>10.00</Amount>

<CurrencyCode>USD</CurrencyCode>

<FormattedPrice>$10.00</FormattedPrice>

</Reward>

<AutoApprovalDelayInSeconds>2592000</AutoApprovalDelayInSeconds>

<Expiration>2016-09-08T00:16:21Z</Expiration>

<AssignmentDurationInSeconds>30</AssignmentDurationInSeconds>

<NumberOfAssignmentsPending>0</NumberOfAssignmentsPending>

<NumberOfAssignmentsAvailable>1</NumberOfAssignmentsAvailable>

<NumberOfAssignmentsCompleted>0</NumberOfAssignmentsCompleted>

</HIT>

</SearchHITsResult>

Conclusion

We have come to the end of this book. Amazon Mechanical MTurkey is a good tool and website created by Amazon which can help one earn some money for carrying out small tasks. The two parties involved on the site are the Requesters and the workers. The Requesters are the individuals who need their tasks to be done, that is, they have the tasks and they are looking for someone to perform them. The tasks are usually referred to as "Human Intelligent Tasks (HITs)" and the Requester has to create them on the Mechanical Turk website.

The workers usually search for the HITs. One has to select the HITs which they prefer. The good thing with MTurk is that there are scripts which can help your work easier. These scripts help the workers to automate most of their tasks, and they in turn earn more from MTurk. You can use scripts to track the HITs posted by your favorite

Requesters, and you will always work for them. Feel free to use scripts which will help you track your work and earnings, and this will be useful to you. However, before installing a particular script, be sure that it is secure. Information about it can be obtained from reviews given by users.

www.ingramcontent.com/pod-product-compliance
Lightning Source LLC
Chambersburg PA
CBHW071803170526
45167CB00003B/1145

* 9 7 8 1 5 4 2 9 7 4 2 6 4 *